CHRISTMAS MOVIE TRIVIA

Publications International, Ltd.

Writers: Lisa Brooks, Amanda Kellogg

Cover art: Shutterstock.com

Louis Weber, CEO
Publications International, Ltd.
8140 Lehigh Avenue
Morton Grove, Illinois 60053

ISBN: 978-1-68022-132-9

Manufactured in Canada.

8 7 6 5 4 3 2

TABLE OF CONTENTS

Continued on next page

A CHARLIE BROWN CHRISTMAS

1. When was A Charlie Brown Christmas first released?

    A. 1964
    B. 1965
    C. 1967
    D. 1969

2. The original broadcast included some animated segments featuring the logo of which sponsor?

    A. Coca-Cola
    B. Ivory Soap
    C. Kellogg's
    D. Campbell Soup

1.

B. 1965

2.

A. Coca-Cola

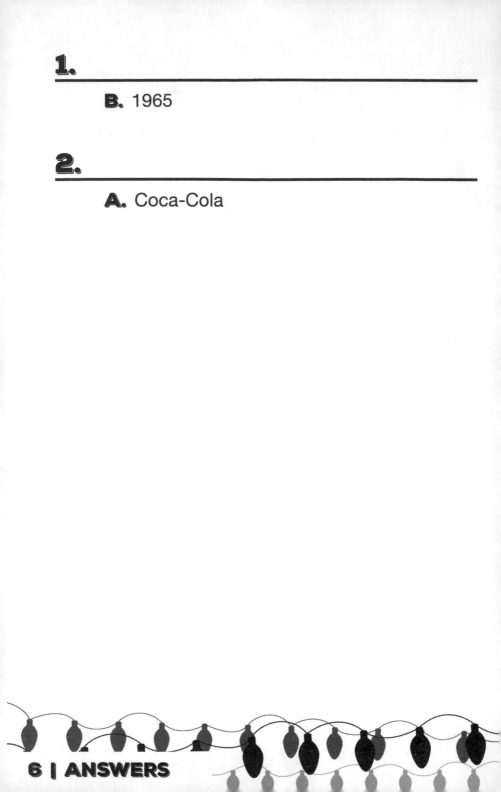

3. The show was the debut for the director, who would later go on to direct an impressive list of Charlie Brown specials. What was his name?

    A. Lee Mendelson
    B. Charles M. Schulz
    C. Vince Guaraldi
    D. Bill Melendez

4. What was the name of the actor who provided the voice of Charlie Brown?

    A. Peter Robbins
    B. Chris Doran
    C. Geoffery Ornstein
    D. Christopher Shea

5. The original broadcast of A Charlie Brown Christmas preempted which show?

    A. I Dream of Jeannie
    B. Gilligan's Island
    C. The Munsters
    D. Bewitched

3.

D. Bill Melendez

4.

A. Peter Robbins

5.

C. The Munsters

6. How much does Lucy charge for her "psychiatric" services?

    A. one penny
    B. five cents
    C. a dime
    D. fifteen cents

7. When Sally dictates a letter to Santa, she ultimately asks for only one thing — what is it?

    A. a pony
    B. a doll
    C. money
    D. world peace

8. From which book of the Bible does Linus recite during his famous speech?

    A. Matthew
    B. Mark
    C. Luke
    D. John

6.

B. five cents

7.

C. money

8.

C. Luke

9. Which Peanuts character does NOT make an appearance in A Charlie Brown Christmas?

    A. Schroeder
    B. Peppermint Patty
    C. Violet
    D. Frieda

10. What does Lucy say she truly wants for Christmas, but never gets?

    A. a bicycle
    B. real estate
    C. money
    D. new clothes

11. When Linus catches a snowflake on his tongue, what does he say it needs?

    A. salt
    B. pepper
    C. sugar
    D. spice

9.

B. Peppermint Patty

10.

B. real estate

11.

C. sugar

12. Lucy asks Charlie Brown if he has pantophobia, and he emphatically answers in the affirmative. Pantophobia is the fear of what?

    A. cats
    B. the ocean
    C. everything
    D. footballs

13. What is Charlie Brown's job in the Christmas pageant?

    A. prop master
    B. choreographer
    C. stagehand
    D. director

14. Which instrument does Snoopy play when the Peanuts gang dances on the stage?

    A. guitar
    B. piano
    C. harmonica
    D. triangle

12.

C. everything

13.

D. director

14.

A. guitar

15. What song does Lucy ask Schroeder to play on his piano?

    A. "Jingle Bells"
    B. "Deck the Halls"
    C. "Silent Night"
    D. "Joy to the World"

16. What kind of tree does Lucy think Charlie Brown should find for the Christmas pageant?

    A. a pine tree
    B. a fir tree
    C. a plastic tree
    D. an aluminum tree

17. Where does the gang find the ornaments to decorate Charlie Brown's sparse little tree?

    A. at Lucy's house
    B. backstage at the Christmas pageant
    C. on Snoopy's doghouse
    D. buried in the snow

18. What is the final song sung in the film?

    A. "Hark the Herald Angels Sing"
    B. "O Christmas Tree"
    C. "Joy to the World"
    D. "Silent Night"

15.

A. "Jingle Bells"

16.

D. an aluminum tree

17.

C. on Snoopy's doghouse

18.

A. "Hark the Herald Angels Sing"

19. TRUE OR FALSE:

Linus holds on to his blanket throughout the entire show.

20. TRUE OR FALSE:

A Charlie Brown Christmas was the first animated Peanuts special.

21. TRUE OR FALSE:

When Lucy and Schroeder are talking about Beethoven, Lucy says that Beethoven wasn't so great because his picture had never been in the newspaper.

22. TRUE OR FALSE:

The children who voiced the Peanuts characters were not listed in the credits at the end of the film.

23. TRUE OR FALSE:

A Charlie Brown Christmas is the longest-running Christmas special on U.S. network television.

19.

FALSE: When Linus recites the biblical Christmas story, he lets go of his blanket. He also lets go of it at the very end of the film, when he uses the blanket to prop up the tiny tree.

20.

TRUE

21.

FALSE: According to Lucy, Beethoven must not have been that great, because his picture has never been on bubblegum cards.

22.

TRUE

23.

FALSE: The show is second only to Rudolph the Red-Nosed Reindeer, which premiered one year earlier.

WHITE CHRISTMAS

1. What year was the classic film White Christmas released?

    A. 1953
    B. 1954
    C. 1955
    D. 1956

2. Unlike many Christmas movies, the film opens in a not-so-cheerful location. Where does the story begin?

    A. in a prison
    B. in an orphanage
    C. in a war-ruined town
    D. in a hospital

1.

B. 1954

2.

C. in a war-ruined town

3. Which crooner played the part of army veteran Bob Wallace?

> **A.** Bing Crosby
> **B.** Frank Sinatra
> **C.** Dean Martin
> **D.** Fred Astaire

4. Danny Kaye appeared as Bob Wallace's army buddy, Phil Davis. But who was originally offered the part?

> **A.** Gene Kelly
> **B.** Jimmy Stewart
> **C.** Tony Martin
> **D.** Fred Astaire

5. Who wrote the famous title song?

> **A.** Ira Gershwin
> **B.** Irving Berlin
> **C.** Stephen Sondheim
> **D.** George Gershwin

3.

A. Bing Crosby

4.

D. Fred Astaire

5.

B. Irving Berlin

6. In addition to "White Christmas" and more than 1,500 other songs, which patriotic standard did the composer also write?

    A. "God Bless America"
    B. "America the Beautiful"
    C. "You're a Grand Old Flag"
    D. "This is My Country"

7. Which popular 1950s recording artist played the part of Betty Haynes?

    A. Doris Day
    B. Judy Garland
    C. Rosemary Clooney
    D. Peggy Lee

8. What is the relationship between song-and-dance partners Betty and Judy?

    A. mother and daughter
    B. cousins
    C. sisters
    D. aunt and niece

6.

   A. "God Bless America"

7.

   C. Rosemary Clooney

8.

   C. sisters

9. In what city do Bob and Phil first see Betty and Judy's act?

    A. Miami
    B. New York
    C. Boston
    D. Atlanta

10. What is the name of the ski lodge where the foursome stays in Vermont?

    A. Village Inn
    B. Pine Tree Hotel
    C. Green Mountain Hotel
    D. Columbia Inn

11. What is unusual about the weather when the group arrives?

    A. it's raining
    B. there is no snow
    C. there is a thunderstorm
    D. it's very windy

9.

A. Miami

10.

D. Columbia Inn

11.

B. there is no snow

12. How do Bob and Phil know the owner of the lodge, Thomas Waverly?

    A. from college
    B. he is Bob's landlord
    C. he was their general in the army
    D. he is Phil's neighbor

13. According to the song that Phil sings, when do the best things happen?

    A. when you're dancing
    B. at night
    C. when you sing
    D. when it snows

14. What is the name of the show on which Bob appears to ask his army buddies to come to Vermont?

    A. The Bill Sullivan Show
    B. The Tonight Show
    C. Entertainment Hour
    D. The Ed Harrison Show

12.

C. he was their general in the army

13.

A. when you're dancing

14.

D. The Ed Harrison Show

15. At the end of the movie, Bob finds Betty's Christmas present to him behind the tree on stage at the Christmas show. What is it?

    A. a book
    B. a framed picture
    C. a statue of a knight on a horse
    D. a winter coat

16. TRUE OR FALSE:
Contrary to the name of the movie, it never ends up snowing during White Christmas.

17. TRUE OR FALSE:
The movie was the first to feature Bing Crosby singing "White Christmas."

18. TRUE OR FALSE:
The movie was the top-grossing film of 1954.

15.

C. a statue of a knight on a horse

16.

FALSE: It does finally snow, but not until the very last moments of the film. The backdrop of the stage at the Christmas show raises, revealing falling snow.

17.

FALSE: White Christmas was the third movie in which Bing Crosby sang the song of the same name. The first two were Holiday Inn and Blue Skies.

18.

TRUE

19. TRUE OR FALSE:

Rosemary Clooney is George Clooney's mother.

20. TRUE OR FALSE:

Although Rosemary Clooney played Vera-Ellen's older sister in the film, in reality she was seven years younger than her costar.

21. TRUE OR FALSE:

The song "White Christmas" was nominated for an Oscar.

22. TRUE OR FALSE:

The silly "Sisters" act that Bing Crosby and Danny Kaye perform was not in the original script. The director added it in after seeing the two actors clowning around on the set.

19.

FALSE: Rosemary is George's aunt.

20.

TRUE

21.

FALSE: While "White Christmas" was overlooked, the song "Count Your Blessings Instead of Sheep" did receive an Oscar nod.

22.

TRUE

A CHRISTMAS STORY

1. In what year was A Christmas Story released?

    A. 1985
    B. 1983
    C. 1982
    D. 1987

2. What is the name of the actor who played Ralphie?

    A. Zack Ward
    B. R.D. Robb
    C. Peter Billingsley
    D. Ian Petrella

1.

B. 1983

2.

C. Peter Billingsley

3. Ralphie mentions his fondest Christmas wish 28 times in the movie. What is it?

    A. a Lone Ranger rifle
    B. a Red Ryder BB gun
    C. a Little Orphan Annie decoder ring
    D. toy soldiers

4. Which actor played "the Old Man"?

    A. Darren McGavin
    B. Jack Nicholson
    C. Roy Scheider
    D. Robert De Niro

5. When Ralphie finally sees Santa at Higbee's department store, he draws a blank. What gift does he reluctantly agree to?

    A. a train set
    B. a cowboy hat
    C. a puppy
    D. a football

6. What is Ralphie's brother's name?

    A. Randy
    B. Bobby
    C. Jimmy
    D. Johnny

3.

 B. a Red Ryder BB gun

4.

A. Darren McGavin

5.

D. a football

6.

A. Randy

7. In which other holiday favorite did Peter Billingsley have an uncredited cameo?

    A. The Santa Clause
    B. Scrooged
    C. Bad Santa
    D. Elf

8. What gift does Ralphie receive from his Aunt Clara?

    A. a stuffed bear
    B. pajamas
    C. a pink bunny suit
    D. a book

9. Why does the Parker family end up having Christmas dinner at a Chinese restaurant?

    A. the oven was broken
    B. the store ran out of turkeys
    C. the electricity went out
    D. the neighbor's dogs ate the turkey

10. Who is the writer and narrator of the film?

    A. Jean Shepherd
    B. Bob Clark
    C. Darren McGavin
    D. Jeff Gillen

7.

D. Elf

8.

C. a pink bunny suit

9.

D. the neighbor's dogs ate the turkey

10.

A. Jean Shepherd

11. A Christmas Story was set in the town of Hammond, Indiana. Which city was used to recreate the town for the film?

    A. Gary, Indiana
    B. Kalamazoo, Michigan
    C. Cleveland, Ohio
    D. Fort Wayne, Indiana

12. Which classmate stuck his tongue to the freezing flagpole on a "triple dog dare"?

    A. Scut Farkus
    B. Flick
    C. Schwartz
    D. Randy

13. What grade does Ralphie get on his theme?

    A. C+
    B. A
    C. B+
    D. C-

11.

C. Cleveland, Ohio

12.

B. Flick

13.

A. C+

14. A Christmas Story features characters from which popular, non-holiday, 1939 movie?

    A. Gone with the Wind
    B. The Adventures of Sherlock Holmes
    C. The Little Princess
    D. The Wizard of Oz

15. When the Old Man receives a lamp in the shape of a leg as a contest prize, he insists it is what?

    A. a fantastic prize
    B. a major award
    C. a huge achievement
    D. a great honor

16. Which brand of soap does Ralphie describe as having "a nice, piquant, after-dinner flavor"?

    A. Lux
    B. Ivory
    C. Palmolive
    D. Lifebuoy

14.

D. The Wizard of Oz

15.

B. a major award

16.

C. Palmolive

17. TRUE OR FALSE:

Wil Wheaton (of Star Trek: The Next Generation fame) auditioned for the part of Ralphie.

18. TRUE OR FALSE:

A fan purchased the house that was used for exterior shots of the Parker home and renovated it to match the look of the home in the movie. It is now open to the public as a museum.

19. TRUE OR FALSE:

Peter Billingsley improvised the ranting dialogue in the scene where Ralphie beats up Scut Farkus.

17.

TRUE

18.

TRUE

19.

FALSE: Although seemingly random and nonsensical, the dialogue was scripted, word for word.

20. TRUE OR FALSE:

The entire movie was filmed in Cleveland, Ohio.

21. TRUE OR FALSE:

In 2012, the film was adapted into a Broadway musical.

22. TRUE OR FALSE:

The director of the movie had a cameo as an irritated man waiting in line to see Santa.

23. TRUE OR FALSE:

A Christmas Story was the inspiration for the television show The Wonder Years.

20.

FALSE: While many exterior shots were filmed in Cleveland, most of the interior shots, as well as the scenes at Ralphie's school, were filmed in Toronto, Ontario.

21.

TRUE

22.

FALSE: The director, Bob Clark, actually had a cameo as the neighbor who marvels at the glowing leg lamp in the window. Jean Shepherd, the writer and narrator, was the man waiting in line for Santa.

23.

TRUE

THE SANTA CLAUSE

1. The director of The Santa Clause, John Pasquin, also directed which movie sequel?

    A. The Santa Clause 2
    B. Miss Congeniality 2: Armed and Fabulous
    C. Home Alone 2: Lost in New York
    D. Die Hard 2

2. What is the original job of the main character, Scott Calvin?

    A. Advertising executive for a toy company
    B. CEO of a large financial corporation
    C. School bus driver
    D. Lawyer

1.

B. Miss Congeniality 2:
Armed and Fabulous

2.

A. Advertising executive for a toy company

3. What is the name of Scott's son?

    A. Bernard
    B. Kevin
    C. George
    D. Charlie

4. Scott discovers Santa Claus on his roof on Christmas Eve. Santa falls, and Scott finds something in his pocket. What is it?

    A. His identification
    B. The naughty or nice list
    C. The Santa Clause
    D. Cookies and carrots for the reindeer

5. What happens when Scott puts on Santa's suit?

    A. He can fly
    B. He becomes Santa Claus
    C. He rips the pants
    D. Charlie convinces him the man on the roof wasn't the real Santa

3.

D. Charlie

4.

C. The Santa Clause

5.

B. He becomes Santa Claus

6. At the end of Scott's first night as the new Santa Claus, he and Charlie end up in the North Pole. The head elf, Bernard, tells Scott he can return home to get his affairs in order but is due back to the North Pole when?

    A. Thanksgiving
    B. Next Christmas
    C. Halloween
    D. Easter

7. Judy the Elf spent 1200 years perfecting her hot cocoa recipe. What is her secret?

    A. Piping hot, a dash of cinnamon, stirred with a candy cane
    B. Not too hot, extra chocolate, shaken not stirred
    C. Extra creamy, a pinch of salt, swirled with vanilla bean
    D. Super sweet, blended with caramel, topped with foam

6.

A. Thanksgiving

7.

B. Not too hot, extra chocolate,
shaken not stirred

8. Scott receives a rather large delivery of many packages. What is in them?

    A. Variations of the Santa Claus suit
    B. Toys to be delivered to the children on Christmas Eve
    C. Letters to Santa Claus
    D. The naughty or nice list

9. What is wrong with the milk Scott drinks at the good little girl's house?

    A. It's chocolate milk
    B. It's past its expiration date
    C. It's soy milk
    D. It doesn't have any cookies to go with it

10. What happens when the police find Scott on Christmas Eve?

    A. They arrest him
    B. They help him deliver the rest of the toys
    C. They give him their letters to Santa
    D. They ask him for Christmas cookies

11. TRUE OR FALSE:
Charlie has an unwavering faith in Santa Claus from the very beginning of the film.

8.

D. The naughty or nice list

9.

C. It's soy milk

10.

A. They arrest him

11.

FALSE: Charlie is skeptical about Santa Claus until he sees proof.

12. TRUE OR FALSE:

Scott initially explains his rapid weight gain by saying he was stung by a bee.

13. TRUE OR FALSE:

On career day, Charlie introduces his dad as Santa Claus to the entire class, causing his mom serious concerns about Scott's mental health.

14. TRUE OR FALSE:

Scott decides to dye his hair stark white so he will match the traditional appearance of Santa Claus.

15. TRUE OR FALSE:

Neil stopped believing in Santa Claus when he wished for a toy train for Christmas but didn't receive the gift.

16. TRUE OR FALSE:

The film The Santa Clause was a box office hit, grossing more than $144 million in the United States and Canada.

17. TRUE OR FALSE:

Bernard gives Charlie a snow globe he can use to see his dad any time he'd like.

12.

TRUE

13.

TRUE

14.

FALSE: Scott's hair miraculously turns white and grows longer, even just moments after being dyed dark and cut short. He instantly grows a beard to match.

15.

FALSE: Neil wanted an Oscar Mayer weenie whistle.

16.

TRUE

17.

TRUE

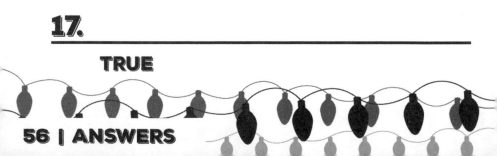

THE SANTA CLAUSE 2

1. What does Scott need in order to remain Santa Claus?

    A. A new reindeer
    B. Christmas spirit
    C. A wife
    D. A legal change of name

2. Who is Lucy?

    A. Scott's daughter
    B. Scott's ex-wife
    C. Charlie's aunt
    D. Charlie's sister

1.

C. A wife

2.

D. Charlie's sister

3. What is Curtis's job?

    A. Keeper of the Handbook of Christmas
    B. Christmas Cookie Captain
    C. Naughty List Double Checker
    D. Official North Pole Matchmaker

4. What shocking news does Scott receive about Charlie?

    A. He no longer believes in Santa Claus
    B. He is on the naughty list
    C. He has run away from home
    D. He wants to work as an elf in the North Pole

5. Scott begins to fall in love with an unlikely person. Who is she?

    A. Charlie's principal
    B. The head elf
    C. Neil's sister
    D. Mother Nature

3.

A. Keeper of the Handbook of Christmas

4.

B. He is on the naughty list

5.

A. Charlie's principal

6. Scott discusses his search for a Mrs. Claus at the Council of Legendary Figures meeting. Who is not among the attendees?

    A. The Sandman
    B. Father Time
    C. Jack Frost
    D. Cupid

7. What does Curtis help Scott create to cover up the fact that he will be away from the North Pole while he searches for his Mrs. Claus?

    A. A Santa Claus hologram
    B. A life-size toy replica of Santa Claus
    C. A voice-emulator Curtis can use to speak to the elves and sound just like Santa Claus
    D. A story about Santa Claus researching the latest in toy technology

8. Where do Scott and Carol go on a date, transported by a magical sleigh ride?

    A. The school Christmas recital
    B. Le Petit Pois, an expensive French restaurant
    C. A casual local pub
    D. The school faculty Christmas party

6.

C. Jack Frost

7.

B. A life-size toy replica of Santa Claus

8.

D. The school faculty Christmas party

9. How does Charlie help convince Carol that Scott really is Santa Claus?

    A. He shows her the naughty or nice list
    B. He reveals that he knows what she wanted for Christmas as a young child
    C. He shows her his magic snow globe
    D. He summons Bernard to explain everything to her

10. TRUE OR FALSE:
The Santa Clause 2 is directed by the same director as The Santa Clause.

11. TRUE OR FALSE:
Principal Newman catches Charlie defacing the walls of the school gymnasium with graffiti.

12. TRUE OR FALSE:
Scott has unlimited magic to help him perform miracles in order to impress and secure a wife.

9.

C. He shows her his magic snow globe

10.

FALSE: The Santa Clause 2 is directed by Michael Lembeck.

11.

TRUE

12.

FALSE: Scott has begun the de-Santa-fication process and he is gradually turning back into his normal self.

13. TRUE OR FALSE:
The Santa Claus replica implements a totalitarian regime over the workshop and declares that every child is on the naughty list.

14. TRUE OR FALSE:
The life-size tin-soldier costumes worn by the actors were made of fiberglass and weighed over 50 pounds each.

15. TRUE OR FALSE:
When Curtis finds Scott to tell him about the evil reign of the Santa Claus replica, they fly back to the North Pole together on Curtis's jetpack.

16. TRUE OR FALSE:
Mother Nature performs Scott and Carol's wedding ceremony.

13.

TRUE

14.

TRUE

15.

FALSE: Curtis's jetpack is broken, so when Lucy loses a tooth, they convince the Tooth Fairy to fly them back to the North Pole.

16.

TRUE

THE SANTA CLAUSE 3: THE ESCAPE CLAUSE

1. What actor portrayed Jack Frost?

    A. Martin Short
    B. Steve Martin
    C. Danny DeVito
    D. Judge Reinhold

2. How much time passes between the second and third movies?

    A. 8 years
    B. 2 years
    C. 4 years
    D. 20 years

1.

A. Martin Short

2.

C. 4 years

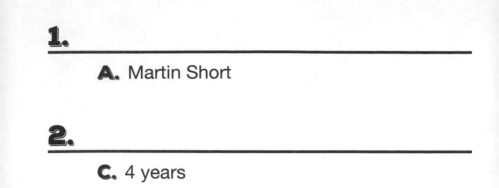

3. What are Scott and Carol expecting at the very beginning of the movie?

    A. Their families for a visit

    B. A baby

    C. A harder than usual Christmas, what with Christmas Spirit at an all-time low

    D. An especially happy Christmas, what with Christmas Spirit at an all-time high

4. Who joins the meeting of the Council of Legendary Figures?

    A. Saint Patrick

    B. Frosty the Snowman

    C. Old Man Winter

    D. Jack Frost

5. Mother Nature accused Jack Frost of a crime. What is it?

    A. Attempting to upstage Santa Claus, in a manner that is both willful and malicious

    B. Bringing winter weather too early, destroying the crops for Christmas fruitcakes

    C. A crime against fashion

    D. Revealing the secrets of other Legendary Figures, blowing their covers

3.

B. A baby

4.

D. Jack Frost

5.

A. Attempting to upstage Santa Claus, in a manner that is both willful and malicious

6. Why does Scott want to decorate the North Pole with items that one would expect to find only in Canada?

    A. The North Pole celebrates a different country every year, and it's Canada's turn

    B. Jack Frost is originally from Nova Scotia and he wants to help him feel at home

    C. Carol's parents are visiting and they believe he's a toymaker in Canada

    D. Lucy is studying geography for a very important upcoming test

7. What special item must Scott hold while wishing he'd never been Santa Claus at all in order to invoke the escape clause?

    A. The Santa Clause card taken from the previous Santa's pocket

    B. A special snow globe that shows Scott Calvin as Santa Claus

    C. The world's largest candy cane

    D. The North Pole itself

6.

C. Carol's parents are visiting and they believe he's a toymaker in Canada

7.

B. A special snow globe that shows Scott Calvin as Santa Claus

8. When Jack Frost becomes the new Santa Claus, he pushes the commercialization of the holiday to its limit. What does he do to the North Pole?

- **A.** He turns it into a multibillion dollar manufacturing plant
- **B.** He closes it completely, insisting that parents should have to buy all the presents while he takes the credit
- **C.** He turns it into a for-profit holiday resort where people can come see the real star of the show—himself!
- **D.** He sells the workshop to the highest bidder, Father Time

9. How does Lucy ultimately unfreeze Jack Frost?

- **A.** She gives him a warm hug
- **B.** She hits him with a blow dryer set on high
- **C.** She sends him on a tropical cruise
- **D.** With a mug of hot cocoa—shaken, not stirred

8.

C. He turns it into a for-profit holiday resort where people can come see the real star of the show—himself!

9.

A. She gives him a warm hug

10. TRUE OR FALSE:
The Santa Clause 3 is the final movie
in the series.

11. TRUE OR FALSE:
The Santa Clause 3 was filmed in
Chicago, IL.

12. TRUE OR FALSE:
When Lucy discovers what Jack Frost is up
to, he freezes her and locks Laura and Neil
in a closet.

13. TRUE OR FALSE:
The Santa Clause 3 was Peter Boyle's final
film to be released before his death

14. TRUE OR FALSE:
In the alternate reality where Scott was never
Santa, Laura and Neil get a divorce.

15. TRUE OR FALSE:
Carol gives birth to a healthy baby girl.

10.

TRUE

11.

FALSE: The movie was filmed mostly in Canada, with a few shots in Los Angeles, California.

12.

FALSE: Jack actually freezes Laura and Neil, and locks Lucy in the closet.

13.

TRUE

14.

TRUE

15.

FALSE: The child is a boy, named Buddy Claus.

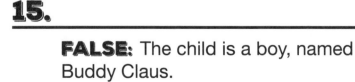

16. Match the quote to the correct movie in the Santa Clause series:

I would caution you all not to point or stare or use the word "plastic."

Fella, if you can hear me, I'm just looking for your identification.

It's time to deliver the packaaaaaage!

Tinsel. Not just for decoration.

You're just a guy who smells like a cookie.

Don't mess with me, Santa. I'm pre-El Nino.

Millions of kids… and they all believe in me, they're counting on me, Charlie.

I would caution you all not to point or stare or use the word "plastic."
–The Santa Clause 2

Fella, if you can hear me, I'm just looking for your identification.
–The Santa Clause

It's time to deliver the packaaaaaage!
 –The Santa Clause 3

Tinsel. Not just for decoration.
–The Santa Clause

You're just a guy who smells like a cookie.
–The Santa Clause 3

Don't mess with me, Santa. I'm pre-El Nino.
–The Santa Clause 2

Millions of kids… and they all believe in me, they're counting on me, Charlie.
–The Santa Clause

THE POLAR EXPRESS

1. The Polar Express is based on a book by which author?

    A. Jonathan Emmett
    B. Chris Van Allsburg
    C. Jan Brett
    D. James Thurber

2. Which Oscar-winner directed the movie?

    A. Steven Spielberg
    B. Peter Jackson
    C. Robert Zemeckis
    D. Tom Hanks

1.

B. Chris Van Allsburg

2.

C. Robert Zemeckis

3. The film's prolific composer has written music for such movies as Back to the Future, The Abyss, and The Avengers. Who is he?

    A. Alan Silvestri
    B. Hans Zimmer
    C. Danny Elfman
    D. James Horner

4. What time is it when the train picks up Hero Boy at his house?

    A. 10:00
    B. 10:45
    C. 11:15
    D. 11:55

5. What is the ultimate destination of the Polar Express?

    A. the Arctic Circle
    B. Mount Everest
    C. Alaska
    D. the North Pole

3.

A. Alan Silvestri

4.

D. 11:55

5.

D. the North Pole

6. Which actor played several parts in the film, including the Conductor, the Hobo, and Santa Claus?

    A. Tom Cruise
    B. Tom Hanks
    C. Brad Pitt
    D. Jim Carrey

7. Only one character on the train is ever mentioned by name: Billy. What other moniker is he given?

    A. Lonely Boy
    B. Hero Boy
    C. Know-It-All
    D. the Conductor

8. What refreshment are the children served on the train?

    A. milk and cookies
    B. gingerbread
    C. hot chocolate
    D. fruitcake

6.

B. Tom Hanks

7.

A. Lonely Boy

8.

C. hot chocolate

9. What is on the track that forces the train to stop?

    A. moose
    B. caribou
    C. elk
    D. reindeer

10. When Hero Boy and the Hobo are on top of the train chasing after Hero Girl, what do they use to traverse the snowy roof?

    A. skis
    B. snowshoes
    C. a sled
    D. snow boots

11. The train encounters "the steepest downhill grade in the world." What is it called?

    A. Glacier Pass
    B. Arctic Mountain
    C. North Pole Gulch
    D. Glacier Gulch

9. _____

B. caribou

10. _____

A. skis

11. _____

D. Glacier Gulch

12. Which famous singer makes a cameo appearance as an elf in a rock band at the North Pole?

    A. Mick Jagger
    B. Paul McCartney
    C. Steven Tyler
    D. Jon Bon Jovi

13. Hero Boy is chosen to receive the first gift of Christmas. What is his gift?

    A. a silver sleigh bell
    B. a red bow
    C. Santa's hat
    D. a toy model of the Polar Express

14. What does the Conductor punch into Hero Boy's ticket?

    A. Lead
    B. Learn
    C. Depend On
    D. Believe

12.

C. Steven Tyler

13.

A. a silver sleigh bell

14.

D. Believe

15. What does the Conductor punch into Hero Girl's ticket?

    A. Lead
    B. Learn
    C. Depend On
    D. Believe

16. When Hero Boy reaches into his pocket to retrieve the bell, he discovers that it has fallen through a hole and he's lost it. How does he find it again?

    A. He sees it on the floor of the train
    B. Lonely Boy finds it and gives it to him
    C. He discovers it in a box under his Christmas tree
    D. He never finds it again

17. Who can hear the ringing of the sleigh bell?

    A. Children
    B. All who truly believe
    C. Hero Boy's family
    D. Anyone who has traveled on the Polar Express

15.

A. Lead

16.

C. He discovers it in a box under his Christmas tree

17.

B. All who truly believe

18. Who sings the movie's theme song "Believe"?

    A. Michael Buble
    B. Andrea Bocelli
    C. Harry Connick Jr.
    D. Josh Groban

19. TRUE OR FALSE:
The Polar Express is listed in the 2006 Guiness Book of World Records as the first all-digital-capture film.

20. TRUE OR FALSE:
The real name of Hero Boy is never mentioned in the film.

21. TRUE OR FALSE:
The address of Lonely Boy, 11344 Edbrooke, was a random address chosen by the director.

22. TRUE OR FALSE:
The movie had its premiere in New York City.

23. TRUE OR FALSE:
The clock in the North Pole village is based on the Pullman Factory Clock Tower in Chicago.

18.

D. Josh Groban

19.

TRUE

20.

TRUE

21.

FALSE: 11344 Edbrooke was the address of Robert Zemeckis' childhood home in the Roseland neighborhood in Chicago's far south side.

22.

FALSE: The premiere was in Grand Rapids, Michigan, which is author Chris Van Allsburg's hometown.

23.

TRUE

THE HOLIDAY

1. In the movie The Holiday, two women — Iris Simpkins and Amanda Woods — swap homes for the holiday season. Which two actresses appear as the duo?

    A. Amy Adams and Kate Beckinsale
    B. Drew Barrymore and Kate Hudson
    C. Cameron Diaz and Kate Winslet
    D. Renee Zellweger and Natalie Portman

2. Where does Iris work?

    A. library
    B. newspaper
    C. advertising agency
    D. book publisher

1.

C. Cameron Diaz and Kate Winslet

2.

B. newspaper

3. What kind of work does Amanda do?

    A. screenwriting
    B. film editing
    C. producing
    D. movie-trailer editing

4. Where in England is Iris's cottage located?

    A. London
    B. Kent
    C. Surrey
    D. Hampshire

5. What one question does Amanda ask Iris before she decides to swap houses?

    A. How is the weather there?
    B. Are there any men in your town?
    C. How much will this cost?
    D. Do you have nice neighbors?

6. Where is Amanda's house located?

    A. Los Angeles
    B. San Diego
    C. San Francisco
    D. Beverly Hills

3.

D. movie-trailer editing

4.

C. Surrey

5.

B. Are there any men in your town?

6.

A. Los Angeles

7. Who knocks on the door of the cottage the first night Amanda is staying there?

    A. a neighbor
    B. the mailman
    C. Iris's brother
    D. Iris's ex-boyfriend

8. After Iris settles in to Amanda's house, she meets Miles, a friend of Amanda's ex-boyfriend. What is Miles' job?

    A. landscaper
    B. composer
    C. actor
    D. chef

9. What can Amanda not do, no matter how hard she tries?

    A. sing
    B. dance
    C. talk to men
    D. cry

7.

C. Iris's brother

8.

B. composer

9.

D. cry

10. How does Iris meet Arthur, Amanda's elderly neighbor?

    A. they bump into each other at the grocery store
    B. she gives him a ride when his car runs out of gas
    C. she drives him home when he can't remember his address
    D. they meet at a restaurant

11. How does Arthur describe their initial encounter?

    A. a "meet cute"
    B. a happy accident
    C. serendipity
    D. fate

12. Amanda overhears Iris's brother Graham talking to "Sophie" and "Olivia." Who are they?

    A. his ex-girlfriends
    B. his daughters
    C. his sisters
    D. his neighbors

10.

C. she drives him home when he can't remember his address

11.

A. a "meet cute"

12.

B. his daughters

13. What did Arthur do for a living before he retired?

    A. actor
    B. composer
    C. director
    D. screenwriter

14. Who does Olivia compare Amanda to?

    A. a princess
    B. the queen
    C. her Barbie doll
    D. her mom

15. When Miles comes back to the house to see Iris for a second time, what is she doing for Arthur?

    A. throwing him a Hanukkah party
    B. cooking him dinner
    C. washing his clothes
    D. reading to him

16. What is the name of Graham's house?

    A. Hill Cottage
    B. Mill House
    C. Meadow House
    D. Hill House

13.

D. screenwriter

14.

C. her Barbie doll

15.

A. throwing him a Hanukkah party

16.

B. Mill House

17. What worries Arthur the most about attending his lifetime achievement tribute?

    A. giving a speech
    B. seeing people he doesn't know
    C. walking up the stairs to the stage
    D. having to leave his house

18. What special thing does Miles do for Arthur for his tribute?

    A. writes Arthur a theme song
    B. rents a limo to take Arthur to the theater
    C. invites some of Arthur's relatives
    D. writes Arthur's speech for him

19. When Amanda decides to give a long-distance relationship with Graham a try, she returns to Iris's house instead of heading to the airport. What is Graham doing when she gets there?

    A. reading
    B. talking on the phone
    C. chopping wood
    D. crying

17.

C. walking up the stairs to the stage

18.

A. writes Arthur a theme song

19.

D. crying

20. TRUE OR FALSE:

Dustin Hoffman's brief cameo in the movie was unplanned and unscripted. He happened to be driving by the filming location, and because he knew the director, he was added to a scene.

21. TRUE OR FALSE:

Amanda never manages to cry at any point in the film.

22. TRUE OR FALSE:

Amanda and Iris don't meet until the very end of the movie.

23. TRUE OR FALSE:

The interior shots of the houses featured in the movie were filmed inside real houses, chosen because of their unique properties.

24. TRUE OR FALSE:

When Amanda asks Iris if there are any men in her town, she answers, "only one."

20.

TRUE

21.

FALSE: She finally cries in the taxi on the way to the airport when she realizes how much she loves Graham.

22.

TRUE

23.

FALSE: Although the houses look nice enough to move into, the interior of each one was constructed on a set.

24.

FALSE: Iris actually answers "zero."

25. TRUE OR FALSE:

One of the movie trailers Amanda works on was for an actual movie, released the same year as The Holiday, starring James Franco and Lindsey Lohan.

26. TRUE OR FALSE:

The website that Amanda and Iris use, homeexchange.com, is a real website.

27. Match the quote to the character who said it:

I think what I've got is something slightly resembling . . . gumption.

I like this Hugo Boss. He cuts a nice suit!

Iris, if you were a melody . . . I used only the good notes.

A good book, a great film, a birthday card, I weep.

*I need some peace and quiet . . .
or whatever it is people go away for.*

25.

FALSE: The trailer (perhaps fortunately) was for a fake movie.

26.

TRUE

27.

I think what I've got is something slightly resembling… gumption. (Iris)

I like this Hugo Boss. He cuts a nice suit! (Arthur)

Iris, if you were a melody . . . I used only the good notes. (Miles)

A good book, a great film, a birthday card, I weep. (Graham)

I need some peace and quiet . . . or what ever it is people go away for. (Amanda)

SCROOGED

1. Scrooged is a comedic adaptation of what classic story?

    A. The Night Before Christmas
    B. A Christmas Carol
    C. The Best Christmas Pageant Ever
    D. A Christmas Memory

2. What year was the movie released?

    A. 1987
    B. 1990
    C. 1988
    D. 1991

1.

B. A Christmas Carol

2.

C. 1988

3. The director of Scrooged also worked on such classics as Superman and Lethal Weapon. Who is he?

    A. Richard Donner
    B. Joe Dante
    C. Chris Columbus
    D. Ivan Reitman

4. Which actor played the cynical Frank Cross?

    A. Jim Carrey
    B. Tom Hanks
    C. Robin Williams
    D. Bill Murray

5. Frank is a programming executive for which television network?

    A. ABC
    B. IBC
    C. CNN
    D. PBS

3.

A. Richard Donner

4.

D. Bill Murray

5.

B. IBC

6. Which actress played Frank's ex-girlfriend and one true love?

    A. Sigourney Weaver
    B. Laura Linney
    C. Karen Allen
    D. Rene Russo

7. What is the nickname Claire gave Frank when they were dating?

    A. Sweetie
    B. Happy
    C. Lumpy
    D. Grumpy

8. What is wrong with Grace Cooley's son Calvin?
    A. he is deaf
    B. he walks with a limp
    C. he is blind
    D. he is mute

6.

C. Karen Allen

7.

C. Lumpy

8.

D. he is mute

9. When a stagehand tells Frank that he's having a hard time attaching tiny antlers to a mouse's head, how does Frank suggest he attach them?

    A. with staples
    B. with glue
    C. with string
    D. with rubber cement

10. When Frank begins to hallucinate while eating lunch in a restaurant, what does he see in his water glass?

    A. fire
    B. a snake
    C. an eyeball
    D. teeth

11. The Ghost of Christmas Past takes Frank back to 1955. What did young Frank want for Christmas that year?

    A. a toy gun
    B. a bicycle
    C. a cowboy hat
    D. a train set

9.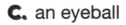

    A. with staples

10.

    C. an eyeball

11.

    D. a train set

12. Where does Frank first meet Claire?

    A. at the office Christmas party
    B. at a Chinese restaurant
    C. on the sidewalk
    D. on the set of a show

13. In his younger life, Frank played the part of a dog on a children's show. What was the dog's name?

    A. Fido
    B. Frisbee
    C. Rex
    D. Rover

14. What gift does Frank give Claire when they are living together?

    A. a set of Ginsu knives
    B. a copy of the Kama Sutra
    C. a book of French poetry
    D. a framed photograph

12.

C. on the sidewalk

13.

B. Frisbee

14.

A. a set of Ginsu knives

15. Which actress played the sprightly, and somewhat violent, Ghost of Christmas Present?

    A. Karen Allen
    B. Carol Kane
    C. Susan Sarandon
    D. Diane Keaton

16. The Ghost of Christmas Present shows Frank that his brother James is playing a game with his friends. Which game are they playing?

    A. Monopoly
    B. Pictionary
    C. Trivial Pursuit
    D. Charades

17. Herman at the homeless shelter mistakes Frank for which actor?

    A. Richard Burton
    B. Lawrence Olivier
    C. Clark Gable
    D. Cary Grant

15.

B. Carol Kane

16.

C. Trivial Pursuit

17.

A. Richard Burton

18. Which Olympian makes a cameo in the movie?

    A. Greg Louganis
    B. Carl Lewis
    C. Mary Lou Retton
    D. Kristi Yamaguchi

19. What object is clutched in Herman's hand when Frank discovers him frozen to death?

    A. a coin
    B. a pocket watch
    C. a bottle of whiskey
    D. a dollar bill

20. Grace replaces the gift Frank wanted to buy for his brother with a VCR. What did Frank actually want to buy?

    A. a towel
    B. a shower curtain
    C. a mug
    D. a picture frame

18.

C. Mary Lou Retton

19.

B. a pocket watch

20.

A. a towel

21. At the end of the film, which character says "God bless us, every one"?

    A. Grace Cooley
    B. Frank Cross
    C. Claire Phillips
    D. Calvin Cooley

22. TRUE OR FALSE:
The role of Eliot Loudermilk was written specifically for Bobcat Goldthwait.

23. TRUE OR FALSE:
Bill Murray's real-life brothers — Bryan Doyle-Murray, John Murray, and Joel Murray — all appear in the movie.

24. TRUE OR FALSE:
When the Ghost of Christmas Future shows Frank the bleak possibility of his death, no one attends his cremation.

21.

D. Calvin Cooley

22.

FALSE: Sam Kinison was originally chosen for the part, but it later went to Goldthwait.

23.

TRUE

24.

FALSE: Only his brother James and sister-in-law Wendie attend his cremation.

25. TRUE OR FALSE:

In the scene when the Ghost of Christmas Present pulls on Frank's lip, Carol Kane grabbed Bill Murray's lip so hard that filming had to stop for several days while his injury healed.

26. TRUE OR FALSE:

The Ghost of Christmas Present tells Frank that Calvin has never spoken a day in his life.

27. TRUE OR FALSE:

Robert Goulet had a cameo as a street musician in the film.

25.

TRUE

26.

FALSE: According to the ghost, Calvin stopped talking when he saw his father killed.

27.

FALSE: Paul Shaffer and Miles Davis both appeared as street musicians. However, Robert Goulet did make an appearance in an IBC network commercial for a show called "Bob Goulet's Old Fashioned Cajun Christmas."

RUDOLPH THE RED-NOSED REINDEER

1. Who is Rudolph's father?

    A. Blitzen
    B. Joe
    C. Donner
    D. Dasher

2. Sam the Snowman welcomes the viewers to the town in the North Pole where Santa and Mrs. Claus live. What does he call it?

    A. Christmastown
    B. Santa's Village
    C. Reindeer Run
    D. Cheertown

1.

C. Donner

2.

A. Christmastown

3. Mrs. Claus is admonishing Santa when we first see them. She exclaims, "Who ever heard of a _____ Santa!"

   A. Stinky
   B. Silly
   C. Skinny
   D. Sad

4. Who narrates the film as the voice of Sam the Snowman, also lending his voice to the movie's soundtrack?

   A. Bing Crosby
   B. Burl Ives
   C. Nat King Cole
   D. Billie Mae Richards

5. The creator of the original Rudolph character, Robert L. May, was charged with creating a Christmas story for which department store?

   A. Macy's
   B. Marshall Field's
   C. Saks Fifth Avenue
   D. Montgomery Ward

3.

    C. Skinny

4.

    B. Burl Ives

5.

    D. Montgomery Ward

6. Johnny Marks, the songster who put May's poem to music, was related to May. What was their relation?

    A. Father and son
    B. Cousins
    C. Brothers-in-law
    D. Uncle and nephew

7. Donner taught Rudolph the ins and outs of being a reindeer in the North Pole. According to Sam, what was the most important thing he taught him?

    A. To beware of the abominable snow monster of the North
    B. To fly
    C. To hide his very shiny nose
    D. To play the reindeer games

8. When Rudolph is at the reindeer games, he catches the eye of a young doe named Clarice. She says she thinks Rudolph is what?

    A. Smart
    B. Cute
    C. Fast
    D. A smooth talker

6.

C. Brothers-in-law

7.

A. To beware of the abominable snow monster of the North

8.

B. Cute

9. When Rudolph and Hermey the elf meet, they decide to be what together?

    A. Dentists
    B. Runaways
    C. Independent
    D. Filled with Christmas cheer

10. Hermey and Rudolph meet a prospector named Yukon Cornelius while on their travels. What color is Cornelius's beard?

    A. Red
    B. Blond
    C. He doesn't have a beard
    D. Brown

11. What is the name of the island the trio stumble upon?

    A. The Island of Toys Moreau
    B. The Island of Misfit Toys
    C. The Island of Forgotten Toys
    D. The Island of Santa's Helpers

9.

C. Independent

10.

A. Red

11.

B. The Island of Misfit Toys

12. Rudolph saves the day by guiding Santa's sleigh on a very foggy Christmas Eve. What song do the elves sing to celebrate?

    A. "Jingle Bells"
    B. "Rudolph the Red-Nosed Reindeer"
    C. "Have a Holly Jolly Christmas"
    D. "The Eye of the Tiger"

13. TRUE OR FALSE:
Santa thinks Rudolph's nose is a useful trait from the very moment he sees it.

14. TRUE OR FALSE:
Hermey would rather be a dentist than a toymaker elf.

12.

C. "Have a Holly Jolly Christmas"

13.

FALSE: At first, Santa doesn't think Rudolph will ever be able to help pull his sleigh.

14.

TRUE

15. TRUE OR FALSE:

The name of the winged lion who looks after the misfit toys is King Moonracer.

16. TRUE OR FALSE:

Cornelius and Hermey ask Rudolph to strike out on his own for fear that his nose will give them all away to the abominable snow monster.

17. TRUE OR FALSE:

Bumbles bounce.

18. TRUE OR FALSE:

Santa doesn't think he'll be able to find homes for all the misfit toys.

15.

TRUE

16.

FALSE: Rudolph decides to leave them in the middle of the night to keep them safe.

17.

TRUE

18.

FALSE: Santa makes a promise to Rudolph that he will find homes for all the misfit toys.

IT'S A WONDERFUL LIFE

1. Who directed It's a Wonderful Life?

    A. Orson Welles
    B. Billy Wilder
    C. Frank Capra
    D. John Huston

2. What is the name of the guardian angel who helps George Bailey realize his true life's worth?

    A. Thomas
    B. Clarence
    C. Gabriel
    D. Ernie

1.

C. Frank Capra

2.

B. Clarence

3. How much money does Uncle Billy misplace on Christmas Eve?

    A. $8,000.00
    B. $2,000.00
    C. $12,000.00
    D. $500.00

4. As George and Mary walk home from the high school dance, they sing the song to which they shared their first dance. What is the song?

    A. "Somewhere, My Love"
    B. "Buffalo Gals"
    C. "The Way You Look Tonight"
    D. "You Are My Sunshine"

5. What are the names of the police officer and cab driver who serenade Mary and George on the night of their wedding?

    A. Simon and Garfunkel
    B. Anthony and Joseph
    C. Bert and Ernie
    D. Charles and John

3.

A. $8,000.00

4.

B. "Buffalo Gals"

5.

C. Bert and Ernie

6. When the Bailey Building and Loan customers panic in the face of a stock market crash and come to collect their money, George pays them from his own pocket. For what special event was that money originally intended?

    A. Zuzu's piano recital
    B. The final payment on the senior Baileys' home
    C. George and Mary's honeymoon
    D. Harry Bailey's welcome home party

7. What happens every time a bell rings?

    A. A prayer is answered
    B. A baby is born
    C. A Christmas wish is made
    D. An angel gets his wings

8. What animal does Uncle Billy keep as a pet at the Bailey Building and Loan?

    A. A dog
    B. A hamster
    C. A raven
    D. A rabbit

6.

C. George and Mary's honeymoon

7.

D. An angel gets his wings

8.

C. A raven

9. What does George find in his pocket while standing on the bridge?

    A. Zuzu's petals
    B. His wedding ring
    C. The keys to his car
    D. Tommy's mitten

10. What is the name of the actress who played Mary Hatch?

    A. Gloria Grahame
    B. Donna Reed
    C. Janet Leigh
    D. Dorothy Dandridge

11. What news distresses the pharmacist, Mr. Gower, so much that he nearly poisons one of his patrons by accident?

    A. Mr. Potter is foreclosing on his home
    B. His wife has filed for divorce
    C. He lost a large sum of money on a bet
    D. His son has died of influenza

9.

A. Zuzu's petals

10.

B. Donna Reed

11.

D. His son has died of influenza

12. Mr. Potter offers George a job in an effort to close down the Bailey Building and Loan. What annual salary does he offer?

    A. $20,000.00
    B. $10,000.00
    C. $45,000.00
    D. $125,000.00

13. What song do the people of Bedford Falls sing while gathered in the Bailey home during the final scene of the film?

    A. "Ode to Joy"
    B. "Auld Lang Syne"
    C. "Deck the Halls"
    D. "Hark! The Herald Angels Sing"

14. TRUE OR FALSE:
It's a Wonderful Life is based on the short story The Greatest Gift by Philip Van Doren Stern.

15. TRUE OR FALSE:
If George Bailey had never been born, the town of Bedford Falls would have become Pottersville.

12.

A. $20,000.00

13.

B. "Auld Lang Syne"

14.

TRUE

15.

TRUE

16. TRUE OR FALSE:
Frank Capra was unhappy with the finished version of the film and refused to attend screenings.

17. TRUE OR FALSE:
George Bailey wanted nothing more than to leave Bedford Falls and explore the world.

18. TRUE OR FALSE:
While sledding with friends, Harry falls through the ice into the freezing river. George saves him, suffering irreparable hearing loss as a result.

19. TRUE OR FALSE:
In the alternate world where George Bailey was never born, Mary Hatch is a school teacher.

20. TRUE OR FALSE:
A large part of the film's budget was devoted to constructing the gym floor at the high school, which opens up over a swimming pool.

16.

FALSE: Director Frank Capra often called It's a Wonderful Life his favorite of all his films.

17.

TRUE

18.

TRUE

19.

FALSE: Mary becomes a librarian.

20.

FALSE: The gym floor and pool were real. The scene was shot at Beverly Hills High School in Los Angeles.

21. TRUE OR FALSE:

A new type of faux snow was created for the film, developed from Foamite, soap, and water. In previous films, artificial snow was made from corn flakes painted white.

22. TRUE OR FALSE:

It's a Wonderful Life was a box office hit, earning twice its production costs in the first week of its release.

23. Match the quote to the character who said it:

Dear George: Remember, no man is a failure who has friends!

Every time a bell rings an angel gets his wings.

I'll give you the moon, Mary.

All you can take with you is that which you've given away.

I'm glad I know you, George Bailey.

George Bailey, whose ship has just come in. Provided he has enough brains to climb aboard.

21.

TRUE

22.

FALSE: While the film is a classic today, it earned only $3.3 million in its initial box office run, while it cost $3.7 million to produce.

23.

Dear George: Remember, no man is a failure who has friends! (Clarence)

Every time a bell rings an angel gets his wings. (ZuZu)

I'll give you the moon, Mary. (George Bailey)

All you can take with you is that which you've given away. (Pa Bailey)

I'm glad I know you, George Bailey. (Violet Bick)

George Bailey, whose ship has just come in. Provided he has enough brains to climb aboard. (Mr. Potter)

PRANCER

1. What is the name of the little girl who befriends the reindeer?

    A. Lisa
    B. Susan
    C. Jessica
    D. Candace

2. What actor played John Riggs, Jessica's father?

    A. Sam Neill
    B. Sam Elliott
    C. James Brolin
    D. Bill Pullman

1.

C. Jessica

2.

B. Sam Elliott

3. Jessica overhears her father talking to her aunt, Sarah, and becomes upset. What are they discussing?

    A. Jessica's brother's struggles in school
    B. A plan to have Jessica live with Sarah
    C. Prancer the reindeer
    D. Not being able to buy Christmas gifts due to financial strain

4. When Jessica and her friend, Carol, are walking home from school, something falls into the street. What is it?

    A. The Prancer decoration from the town's Christmas sleigh display
    B. A streetlight
    C. A Christmas tree
    D. The sign for the reindeer enclosure on the nearby Christmas tree lot

5. How does Jessica determine the fallen reindeer decoration is Prancer?

    A. The name is written on his harness
    B. From the order given in "The Night Before Christmas"
    C. From his coloring
    D. She doesn't, her friend Carol decides the reindeer is Prancer

3.

B. A plan to have Jessica live with Sarah

4.

A. The Prancer decoration from the town's Christmas sleigh display

5.

B. From the order given in "The Night Before Christmas"

6. How does Jessica anger her reclusive neighbor, Mrs. McFarland?

    A. She breaks her window
    B. She sleds through her rose bushes
    C. She allows Prancer to eat her rose bushes
    D. She bumps into her at the grocery store

7. What does Jessica use to entice Prancer out of her father's barn?

    A. hay
    B. a carrot
    C. Christmas cookies
    D. a pie

8. Jessica needs money to buy oats to feed Prancer. What does she do to earn the money?

    A. Works at the grocery store
    B. Cleans her dad's barn
    C. Cleans for Mrs. McFarland
    D. Sells her mother's necklace

6.

B. She sleds through her rose bushes

7.

C. Christmas cookies

8.

C. Cleans for Mrs. McFarland

9. How does the whole town find out about Prancer?

    A. Mrs. McFarland spreads the word
    B. Jessica begins to ask for contributions for his care
    C. Jessica's brother, Steve, tells his teacher
    D. Jessica tells the shopping mall Santa, who relays the story to the editor of the local paper

10. How does Jessica's father find out about Prancer?

    A. Prancer lets the animals out of the barn and enters the Riggs' home
    B. He reads the editorial in the newspaper
    C. Jessica tells him after she becomes overwhelmed with guilt
    D. Jessica's brother, Steve, tells him

D. Jessica tells the shopping mall Santa, who relays the story to the editor of the local paper

10.

A. Prancer lets the animals out of the barn and enters the Riggs' home

11. After learning about Prancer, many townspeople come to the Riggs' farm to see him. They arrive as Jessica's father finds Prancer in his home, and he agrees to sell Prancer to one of them. Who?

    A. The newspaper editor
    B. Jessica's teacher
    C. The local butcher
    D. The veterinarian

12. TRUE OR FALSE:
The name of the real reindeer who portrayed Prancer was Boo.

13. TRUE OR FALSE:
The veterinarian Jessica calls to help the wounded reindeer is happy to help and performs follow up visits to be sure Prancer is doing well.

14. TRUE OR FALSE:
Jessica injures herself at the end of the movie in an ice skating accident.

15. TRUE OR FALSE:
Prancer was released in 1989.

11.

C. The local butcher

12.

TRUE

13.

FALSE: The vet is unwilling to help a wild animal, but relents after Jessica claims doctors never make anyone better.

14.

FALSE: Jessica injures herself trying to free Prancer, who is on display at the local butcher's Christmas tree lot.

15.

TRUE

16. TRUE OR FALSE:

By the end of the film, Jessica realizes the reindeer she has been caring for is not Santa's Prancer.

17. TRUE OR FALSE:

Mrs. McFarland was played by Oscar winning actress Cloris Leachman.

18. TRUE OR FALSE:

The title of the newspaper article about Prancer is "Yes, Santa, there are still Virginias."

19. TRUE OR FALSE:

While Prancer is inside the Riggs' home, he eats all of Jessica's Christmas cookies.

16.

FALSE: Jessica and her father take Prancer to Antler Ridge to release the rehabilitated animal back into the wild. He mysteriously disappears over the edge of the cliff . . . and they see a streak of light, presumed to be Prancer, join Santa's sleigh.

17.

TRUE

18.

TRUE

19.

FALSE: Prancer eats a pie.

ELF

1. Who directed Elf?

    A. J.J. Abrams
    B. Will Ferrell
    C. Jon Favreau
    D. Vince Vaughn

2. What is the name of the lead character?

    A. Timmy
    B. Johnny
    C. Bob
    D. Buddy

1.

C. Jon Favreau

2.

D. Buddy

3. Buddy is an orphaned human infant who accidentally winds up in the North Pole after crawling into Santa's sack on Christmas Eve. Who raises Buddy?

    A. Father Time
    B. Papa Elf
    C. Santa Claus
    D. Mrs. Claus

4. What is the name of the actor who played Santa Claus?

    A. Ed Asner
    B. James Caan
    C. Bob Newhart
    D. Peter Dinklage

5. What is the "Kringle 3000"?

    A. Santa's computer
    B. Buddy's high-tech robotic toy-making invention
    C. A 500-reindeer power jet engine used to power Santa's sleigh
    D. Papa Elf's favorite sandwich

3.

B. Papa Elf

4.

A. Ed Asner

5.

C. A 500-reindeer power jet engine used to power Santa's sleigh

6. How does Buddy find out he is a human and not an elf?

> **A.** He finds a photo of his birth parents in Papa Elf's desk
> **B.** He overhears two other elves talking about him
> **C.** Santa decides Buddy is old enough to handle the truth
> **D.** He gradually realizes he is nothing like the other elves and must be human

7. Who convinces Buddy he should go to New York to find his birth father?

> **A.** Leon the Snowman
> **B.** Poppy the Puffin
> **C.** Ella the Elf
> **D.** Santa Claus

8. As Buddy is leaving the North Pole, his friends are startled by a well-wisher. Who startles them?

> **A.** Papa Elf
> **B.** Buddy's birth father
> **C.** Mr. Narwhal
> **D.** Mrs. Claus

6.

B. He overhears two other elves talking about him

7.

A. Leon the Snowman

8.

C. Mr. Narwhal

9. The design for Santa's workshop in Elf is based on which classic holiday film?

    A. Rudolph the Red-Nosed Reindeer
    B. Frosty the Snowman
    C. Miracle on 34th Street
    D. Santa Claus Is Coming to Town

10. When Buddy finds his father's office, who does his father think he is?

    A. A delivery man
    B. A singing telegram
    C. A summons officer
    D. His son's teacher

11. What is Buddy's father's name?

    A. Harold Thompson
    B. Warren Hobarth
    C. Walter Hobbs
    D. Harrison Jackson

9.

A. Rudolph the Red-Nosed Reindeer

10.

B. A singing telegram

11.

C. Walter Hobbs

12. The elves try to stick to the four main food groups. What are they?

    A. Gumdrops, lollipops, licorice, and gum.
    B. Candy, candy canes, candy corn, and syrup.
    C. Cookies, cake, brownies, and pie.
    D. Pizza, sandwiches, ice cream, and candy.

13. Walter is a professional in which industry?

    A. Advertising
    B. Media sales
    C. Higher education
    D. Publishing

14. Where does Buddy meet Jovie?

    A. Gimbels
    B. Ray's Pizza
    C. Walter's office
    D. The North Pole

12.

B. Candy, candy canes, candy corn,
and syrup.

13.

D. Publishing

14.

A. Gimbels

15. Who gives Buddy the advice to ask Jovie out on a date "to eat food"?

    A. Leon
    B. Michael
    C. Walter
    D. Emily

16. Walter is in danger of losing his job, so he and his team bring in a famous and finicky children's book author to help with ideas. Buddy mistakes the writer, Miles Finch, for what?

    A. A child
    B. A law officer
    C. An elf
    D. Walter's assistant

17. On Christmas Eve, Santa crashes and needs Buddy's help to fix his sleigh. In addition to a fixed engine, what else does Santa say the sleigh needs in order to fly?

    A. Milk and cookies
    B. Reindeer power
    C. Christmas spirit
    D. A new coat of paint

15.

B. Michael

16.

C. An elf

17.

C. Christmas spirit

18. What does Michael want for Christmas?

   A. A Red Ryder BB gun
   B. A new pair of skates
   C. For Buddy to be a part of the family
   D. A real HUF skateboard

19. TRUE OR FALSE:
Buddy believes he is an elf until he reaches adulthood.

20. TRUE OR FALSE:
When Buddy becomes very discouraged with his toy making ability, he claims he is nothing but a "super silly dummy brains."

21. TRUE OR FALSE:
Jovie is full of holiday cheer when she meets Buddy.

22. TRUE OR FALSE:
Elf is the first movie Will Ferrell starred in after leaving Saturday Night Live in 2002.

18.

D. A real HUF skateboard

19.

TRUE

20.

FALSE: Buddy says he is a "cotton headed ninny muggins."

21.

FALSE: Jovie says she is just trying to get through the holidays.

22.

TRUE

23. TRUE OR FALSE:

Will Ferrell pushed to make a sequel to Elf, but the studio rejected the idea.

24. TRUE OR FALSE:

Buddy prepares a healthy and well balanced lunch for Emily to take with her to work.

25. TRUE OR FALSE:

Buddy and Walter eventually bond, helped by Santa's appearance on Christmas Eve.

26. Match the event to the setting where it took place:

Santa crashes his sleigh and loses the sleigh's engine.

Buddy tries coffee for the first time.

Buddy prepares an elaborate welcome for Santa.

Michael and Buddy decorate an oversized Christmas tree.

Buddy and Jovie share their first kiss.

Baby Susie meets Papa Elf.

23.

FALSE: Will Ferrell turned down the opportunity to work on a sequel.

24.

FALSE: Buddy gives Emily a bag of spaghetti covered in maple syrup.

25.

TRUE

26.

Santa crashes his sleigh and loses the sleigh's engine. -Central Park

Buddy tries coffee for the first time. -Walter's office

Buddy prepares an elaborate welcome for Santa. -Gimbels

Michael and Buddy decorate an oversized Christmas tree. -The Hobbs' home

Buddy and Jovie share their first kiss. -Rockefeller Center

Baby Susie meets Papa Elf. -The North Pole

A CHRISTMAS CAROL

1. Who wrote the original novella A Christmas Carol?

- **A.** Herman Melville
- **B.** Mary Shelley
- **C.** Charles Dickens
- **D.** Henry James

2. Approximately how many film adaptations of the story have been produced?

- **A.** 40
- **B.** 60
- **C.** 75
- **D.** more than 80

1.

C. Charles Dickens

2.

D. more than 80

3. Many movie adaptations are set in the same time frame in which the original story was published. What year was this?

    A. 1820
    B. 1843
    C. 1901
    D. 1925

4. In what city does the story take place?

    A. New York
    B. Boston
    C. London
    D. Edinburgh

5. One of the most famous movie versions of A Christmas Carol was released in 1951. Who starred as Ebenezer Scrooge?

    A. Alastair Sim
    B. George C. Scott
    C. Reginald Owen
    D. Walter Matthau

3.

B. 1843

4.

C. London

5.

A. Alastair Sim

6. The story opens on Christmas Eve. Seven years earlier, what event had taken place on this date?

    A. Scrooge started his business
    B. an epic blizzard crippled the city
    C. Scrooge's business partner died
    D. Tiny Tim was born

7. What does the word "humbug" actually mean?

    A. a distasteful event
    B. deceptive or false talk or behavior
    C. one who lacks common sense
    D. a lack of concern or sympathy

8. What was the name of Ebenezer Scrooge's business partner?

    A. Robert Murphy
    B. Bob Cratchit
    C. Jacob Marley
    D. Timothy Cratchit

6.

C. Scrooge's business partner died

7.

B. deceptive or false talk or behavior

8.

C. Jacob Marley

9. Which Oscar winner played Scrooge in a 1984 television adaptation?

    A. George C. Scott
    B. Marlon Brando
    C. Jimmy Stewart
    D. Jack Nicholson

10. What is the name of the downtrodden clerk who works for Scrooge?

    A. Jacob Marley
    B. Fred Marley
    C. Robert Murphy
    D. Bob Cratchit

11. Who is the first ghost to visit Scrooge?

    A. Christmas Yet to Come
    B. Christmas Past
    C. his former business partner
    D. Christmas Present

12. When the first ghost visits, where does it first appear?

    A. in the embers of a fire
    B. in Scrooge's door knocker
    C. in a glass of wine
    D. in a window pane

9.

A. George C. Scott

10.

D. Bob Cratchit

11.

C. his former business partner

12.

B. in Scrooge's door knocker

13. Which Star Trek actor played Scrooge in a 1999 television version of the story?

    A. Patrick Stewart
    B. William Shatner
    C. Leonard Nimoy
    D. Brent Spiner

14. Scrooge's nephew invites him to Christmas dinner. What is his nephew's name?

    A. Bob
    B. Fred
    C. Tim
    D. John

15. The Ghost of Christmas Past reminds Scrooge of his previous engagement to a woman named what?

    A. Christine
    B. Elizabeth
    C. Mary
    D. Belle

13.

A. Patrick Stewart

14.

B. Fred

15.

D. Belle

16. In the 1999 television adaptation, which Broadway actor played the Ghost of Christmas Past?

    A. Nathan Lane
    B. Alan Cumming
    C. Joel Grey
    D. Gary Beach

17. When the ghost of Scrooge's business partner appears to him, what is the ghost covered with?

    A. chains
    B. rags
    C. dirt
    D. snow

18. What was the name of Scrooge's employer when he was young?

    A. Finnigan
    B. Fezziwig
    C. Ferdinand
    D. Fitzwell

16.

C. Joel Grey

17.

A. chains

18.

B. Fezziwig

19. Which actor starred in the 2009 animated movie version of the story?

    A. Tom Hanks
    B. Will Ferrell
    C. Jim Carrey
    D. Hugh Laurie

20. Where does the Ghost of Christmas Present take Scrooge?

    A. to Bob Cratchit's house
    B. to Scrooge's office
    C. to an orphanage
    D. to a hospital

21. What does the Ghost of Christmas Present predict concerning Tiny Tim?

    A. he will be healed
    B. his chair will be empty in a year
    C. he will grow to be strong
    D. he will soon lose the use of his arms

19.

C. Jim Carrey

20.

A. to Bob Cratchit's house

21.

B. his chair will be empty in a year

22. In the 2009 animated version, which Oscar nominee appeared as Bob Cratchit?

    A. Colin Firth
    B. Johnny Depp
    C. Gary Oldman
    D. Jeremy Renner

23. What does the Ghost of Christmas Yet to Come show Scrooge that finally convinces him to change his ways?

    A. the grave of Tiny Tim
    B. all of the people Scrooge has wronged
    C. a vision of Scrooge living on the street
    D. Scrooge's own grave

24. What does Scrooge anonymously send to Bob Cratchit's house on Christmas Day?

    A. gifts for his family
    B. a prize turkey
    C. a Christmas goose
    D. money

22.

C. Gary Oldman

23.

D. Scrooge's own grave

24.

B. a prize turkey

25. Who delivers the famous line, "God bless us, every one"?

   A. Scrooge
   B. Bob Cratchit
   C. Tiny Tim
   D. Fred

26. TRUE OR FALSE:
Just like in the original story, in the majority of film adaptations of A Christmas Carol, the Ghost of Christmas Yet to Come never speaks.

27. TRUE OR FALSE:
Ebenezer Scrooge was an only child.

28. TRUE OR FALSE:
At the end of the story, Scrooge attends Christmas dinner at Bob Cratchit's home.

29. TRUE OR FALSE:
The animated Scrooge from the 2009 version of the story also appeared in The Polar Express as a marionette.

30. TRUE OR FALSE:
The 1999 television version of the story is the only film adaptation to show Jacob Marley's funeral.

25.

C. Tiny Tim

26.

TRUE

27.

FALSE: Scrooge had a sister named Fan.

28.

FALSE: Scrooge goes to his nephew Fred's home for Christmas dinner, after previously rebuffing his invitation.

29.

TRUE

30.

TRUE

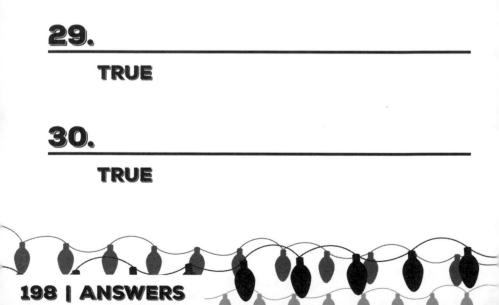

31. TRUE OR FALSE:
The Ghost of Christmas Present is usually represented as a small, elderly man.

32. TRUE OR FALSE:
Although most movie versions of A Christmas Carol depict Ebenezer Scrooge as some sort of money-lender or banker, the original story never specifically mentions his occupation.

33. TRUE OR FALSE:
Charles Dickens chose the name "Scrooge" for his character because it is synonymous with "stingy."

34. TRUE OR FALSE:
The production team from the 1984 television adaptation left a headstone marked "Ebenezer Scrooge" in the graveyard of St. Chad's Church in Shrewsbury, England. It is still there today.

31.

FALSE: Most versions of the story show the Ghost of Christmas Present as a giant, jovial man.

32.

TRUE

33.

FALSE: In Dickens' time, the word was actually a slang term that meant "to squeeze."

34.

TRUE

NATIONAL LAMPOON'S CHRISTMAS VACATION

1. Christmas Vacation was written by John Hughes. Which other holiday favorite did he write?

    A. Scrooged
    B. The Santa Clause
    C. Elf
    D. Home Alone

2. How many lights does Clark Griswold use to light up the house?

    A. 5,000
    B. 15,000
    C. 25,000
    D. 50,000

1.

D. Home Alone

2.

C. 25,000

3. During the movie, an advent calendar counts down the days to Christmas Eve. What is the first day we see opened on the calendar?

    A. December 14
    B. December 9
    C. December 20
    D. December 1

4. What are the names of the yuppie couple who live next door to the Griswolds?

    A. Ted and Margaret
    B. Todd and Margo
    C. Tom and Mary
    B. Tim and Martha

5. Clark is anxiously awaiting his yearly bonus. What does he plan to do with the money?

    A. Take a vacation
    B. Invest in the stock market
    C. Install a pool
    D. Buy a car

3.

A. December 14

4.

B. Todd and Margo

5.

C. Install a pool

6. Doris Roberts, who played Ellen's mother in Christmas Vacation, went on to play another mother in which popular '90s sitcom?

    A. Seinfeld
    B. Friends
    C. Frasier
    D. Everybody Loves Raymond

7. From which state is the license plate on Eddie and Catherine's RV?

    A. Nevada
    B. Iowa
    C. Kansas
    D. Nebraska

8. What were two of the "gifts" that Aunt Bethany wrapped and brought to the house on Christmas Eve?

    A. a cat and a Jell-O mold
    B. a Santa hat and a lightbulb
    C. a cat and a can of cat food
    D. a hat and a can opener

6.

D. Everybody Loves Raymond

7.

C. Kansas

8.

A. a cat and a Jell-O mold

9. Who played Clark's boss, Frank Shirley?

    A. John Lithgow
    B. Bob Gunton
    C. Brian Doyle-Murray
    D. John Heard

10. Several times in the film, Clark is seen wearing a sports team logo hat. Which team is it?

    A. Chicago White Sox
    B. Chicago Blackhawks
    C. Chicago Cubs
    D. Chicago Bears

11. Which Seinfeld regular had a role as one of the aggravated next-door neighbors?

    A. Jerry Seinfeld
    B. Julia Louis-Dreyfus
    C. Jason Alexander
    D. Michael Richards

9.

C. Brian Doyle-Murray

10.

D. Chicago Bears

11.

B. Julia Louis-Dreyfus

12. What does Clark do to pass the time while he's stuck in the attic?

    A. Looks through photo albums
    B. Listens to Christmas music
    C. Watches old family movies
    D. Reads a book

13. Johnny Galecki, who played Rusty, went on to feature in both Roseanne and which other popular sitcom?

    A. Modern Family
    B. The Big Bang Theory
    C. 30 Rock
    D. How I Met Your Mother

14. What does Aunt Bethany recite when she is asked to say grace before Christmas Eve dinner?

    A. the Pledge of Allegiance
    B. the Lord's Prayer
    C. a shopping list
    D. her phone number

12.

C. Watches old family movies

13.

B. The Big Bang Theory

14.

A. the Pledge of Allegiance

15. After Clark covers his sled with an experimental "non-caloric silicon-based kitchen lubricant" and rockets out of control, he finally ends up stopping in the parking lot of which store?

    A. Target
    B. Home Depot
    C. Sears
    D. Wal-Mart

16. Which crooner sings "Mele Kalikimaka" during Clark's pool fantasy sequence?

    A. Bing Crosby
    B. Frank Sinatra
    C. Robert Goulet
    D. Dean Martin

17. Instead of the cash bonus he's expecting, what gift does Clark receive from his boss?

    A. a magazine subscription
    B. a year-long gym membership
    C. a gift certificate
    D. a subscription to a "jelly of the month" club

15.

D. Wal-Mart

16.

A. Bing Crosby

17.

D. a subscription to a "jelly of the month" club

18. How does Frank Shirley react after being kidnapped by Cousin Eddie and confronted by the Griswold family?

    A. he immediately wants to press charges

    B. he doesn't press charges, but refuses to change

    C. he reinstates the bonuses and gives Clark an extra 20 percent

    D. he punches Cousin Eddie and runs

19. TRUE OR FALSE:
The movie ends on Christmas Eve, so we never actually see Christmas day at the Griswold house.

20. TRUE OR FALSE:
Cousin Eddie's son Rocky doesn't have a single line in the film.

21. TRUE OR FALSE:
The movie had a very low budget.

22. TRUE OR FALSE:
In 1989, only two Christmas-themed movies were released: Christmas Vacation and Prancer. Johnny Galecki was in both of them.

18.

C. he reinstates the bonuses and gives Clark an extra 20 percent

19.

TRUE

20.

TRUE

21.

FALSE: The movie actually had an impressive budget for a comedy: $27 million. This is particularly high considering it had very few special effects.

22.

TRUE

23. TRUE OR FALSE:

Mae Questel, who played Aunt Bethany, was the original voice of Minnie Mouse in the 1930s.

24. TRUE OR FALSE:

The home used for the next-door neighbors, which is part of the Warner Brothers Studio back lot, was the same home used for Roger Murtaugh's family in Lethal Weapon.

25. TRUE OR FALSE:

Clark uses twenty different words to describe his boss during his epic, angry rant.

26. TRUE OR FALSE:

In one scene, Clark is trying to read a People magazine with sap-sticky fingers. The person pictured on the cover is the movie's director, Jeremiah Chechik.

23.

FALSE: Mae Questel actually provided the voice for Betty Boop and Olive Oyl.

24.

TRUE

25.

FALSE: It takes thirty words for Clark to truly get his frustration out.

26.

FALSE: The person on the cover is actually one of the movie's executive producers, Matty Simmons.

HOW THE GRINCH STOLE CHRISTMAS

1. How the Grinch Stole Christmas is based on a story by which beloved children's book author?

    A. Roald Dahl
    B. E.B. White
    C. Dr. Seuss
    D. Chris Van Allsburg

2. The director of the film also worked on the production of cartoons such as The Bugs Bunny Show. Who is he?

    A. Chuck Jones
    B. Mel Blanc
    C. Friz Freleng
    D. Robert McKimson

1.

C. Dr. Seuss

2.

A. Chuck Jones

3. Which actor, famous for his roles in classic horror films, narrates the film and provides the voice of the Grinch?

    A. Lon Chaney
    B. Boris Karloff
    C. Vincent Price
    D. Bela Lugosi

4. What is "the most likely reason" that the Grinch hates Christmas so much?

    A. His shoes were too tight
    B. His heart was too cold
    C. His heart was two sizes too small
    D. His head was not screwed on just right

5. How many years has the Grinch been putting up with Christmas in Whoville?

    A. 53
    B. 50
    C. 52
    D. 60

3.

B. Boris Karloff

4.

C. His heart was two sizes too small

5.

A. 53

6. What part of Christmas does the Grinch "hate most of all"?

    A. the presents
    B. the decorations
    C. the food
    D. the singing

7. What is the name of the Grinch's dog?

    A. Spot
    B. Max
    C. Rex
    D. Fido

8. What is the name of the mountain where the Grinch lives?

    A. Mount Crumpit
    B. Who Mountain
    C. Mount Grumpy
    D. Lonely Mountain

9. What is the very first thing the Grinch steals?

    A. a tree
    B. the roast beast
    C. stockings
    D. presents

6.

D. the singing

7.

B. Max

8.

A. Mount Crumpit

9.

C. stockings

10. Which food was NOT on the list of delicacies the Grinch stole from the Who's ice box?

    A. Who hash
    B. Who pudding
    C. Roast beast
    D. Who plums

11. What reason does the Grinch give to Cindy Lou Who when she asks him why he's taking the tree?

    A. it needs more ornaments
    B. one of the lights is broken
    C. he's going to replace it with a bigger tree
    D. the branches are full of sticky sap

12. What is the last thing the Grinch steals from Cindy Lou's house?

    A. the food from the ice box
    B. the presents
    C. the tree
    D. the log for the fire

10.

D. Who plums

11.

B. one of the lights is broken

12.

D. the log for the fire

13. How do the residents of Whoville react when they wake up on Christmas morning and realize all of their things have been stolen?

    A. they gather in the square to sing
    B. they cry
    C. they call the Whoville police
    D. they start searching for their things

14. How many sizes does the Grinch's heart grow on Christmas Day?

    A. 2
    B. 3
    C. 4
    D. 5

15. TRUE OR FALSE:
Boris Karloff, who narrated the film, sang "You're a Mean One, Mr. Grinch."

16. TRUE OR FALSE:
Dr. Seuss had been hoping to animate one of his books for some time.

17. TRUE OR FALSE:
The Grinch has always been green.

13.

A. they gather in the square to sing

14.

B. 3

15.

FALSE: The famous song was performed by Thurl Ravenscroft, who was also the voice of Tony the Tiger.

16.

FALSE: The author was uninterested in translating one of his books into an animated form, but Chuck Jones eventually convinced him.

17.

FALSE: The original Grinch in Dr. Seuss's book was black and white.

18. TRUE OR FALSE:

Dr. Seuss wrote the lyrics for the songs in the film.

19. TRUE OR FALSE:

The words to the song "Fahoo Fores" were written to sound like classical Latin, and some viewers of the film actually requested translations.

20. "You're a Mean One, Mr. Grinch" is the antithesis of most cheery Christmas songs. It contains dozens of insults, hurled at the deplorable Mr. Grinch. Which of the following are included (yes) or not included (no) in the song?

Your soul is filled with wasps
You have termites in your smile
You're an abominable cad
You're a foul one
Your heart is full of unwashed socks
You're a crooked, dirty jockey
Your heart's a lump of coal
You nauseate me
Your soul is an appalling dump heap
You have fleas in your brain
Your heart's a dead tomato

18.

TRUE

19.

TRUE

20.

Your soul is filled with wasps (no)

You have termites in your smile (yes)

You're an abominable cad (no)

You're a foul one (yes)

Your heart is full of unwashed socks (yes)

You're a crooked, dirty jockey (yes)

Your heart's a lump of coal (no)

You nauseate me (yes)

Your soul is an appalling dump heap (yes)

You have fleas in your brain (no)

Your heart's a dead tomato (yes)

HOME ALONE

1. What year was Home Alone released?

    A. 1989
    B. 1990
    C. 1991
    D. 1992

2. Which director, famous for his work on The Goonies and Gremlins, directed the movie?

    A. Richard Donner
    B. Steven Spielberg
    C. John Hughes
    D. Chris Columbus

1.

B. 1990

2.

D. Chris Columbus

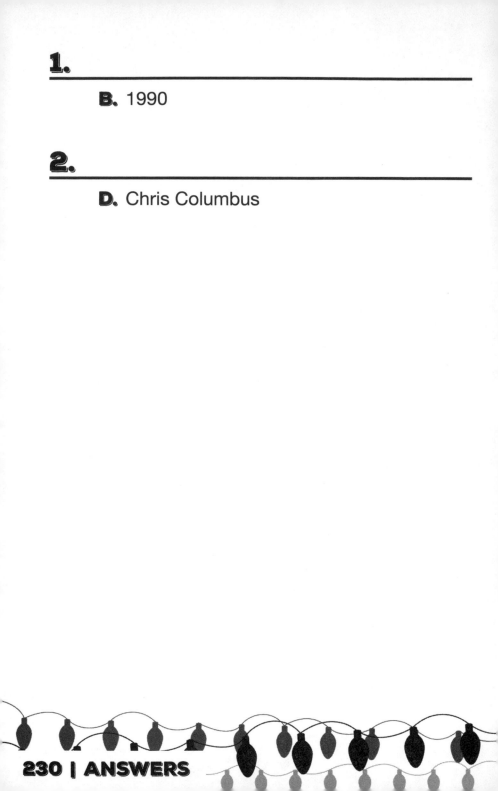

3. The film's composer has written some of the
   most recognizable music in film history.
   Who is he?

   A. Hans Zimmer
   B. James Horner
   C. John Williams
   D. Henry Mancini

4. The McCallisters live in the suburbs of which
   major city?

   A. New York
   B. Chicago
   C. Minneapolis
   D. Los Angeles

5. Macaulay Culkin's real brother, Kieran Culkin,
   played who in the movie?

   A. Buzz
   B. Jeff
   C. Fuller
   D. the stock boy at the drug store

3.

    C. John Williams

4.

    B. Chicago

5.

    C. Fuller

6. How old is Kevin?

A. 7
B. 8
C. 9
D. 10

7. What is Kevin's father's name?

A. Peter
B. John
C. Henry
D. David

8. Which city are the McCallisters traveling to for Christmas?

A. New York
B. Rome
C. Miami
D. Paris

9. How many kids are staying in the McCallister house before they leave for the airport?

A. 10
B. 11
C. 12
D. 13

6.

B. 8

7.

A. Peter

8.

D. Paris

9.

B. 11

10. What is Kevin's favorite pizza topping?

    A. pepperoni
    B. mushrooms
    C. cheese
    D. sausage

11. Why are the kids afraid of the neighbor, Old Man Marley?

    A. he yells at them
    B. they think he's a kidnapper
    C. he owns a gun
    D. they think he killed his family

12. Kevin orders his "very own cheese pizza" from which restaurant?

    A. Pizza Hut
    B. Little Nero's
    C. Domino's
    D. Papa John's

13. Before it went to Joe Pesci, which actor turned down the role of Harry?

    A. Robert De Niro
    B. Al Pacino
    C. Gary Oldman
    D. Jim Carrey

10.

C. cheese

11.

D. they think he killed his family

12.

B. Little Nero's

13.

A. Robert De Niro

14. When Kevin goes to see Santa, what does he ask for?

    A. peace on earth
    B. a safe trip for his family
    C. protection from the burglars
    D. the return of his family

15. Which actor, who filmed his entire part in one day, appears in the film as a polka player who helps Kevin's mom?

    A. John Candy
    B. John Belushi
    C. John Goodman
    D. Dan Aykroyd

16. Why does Kevin end up stealing a toothbrush from the drugstore?

    A. He runs out of money
    B. He forgets to pay
    C. Old Man Marley comes into the store and scares him
    D. He's upset that the toothbrush isn't approved by the ADA

14.

D. the return of his family

15.

A. John Candy

16.

C. Old Man Marley comes into the store and scares him

17. Which item does Kevin NOT buy at the store?

    A. milk
    B. eggnog
    C. orange juice
    D. fabric softener

18. Marv leaves the water running in all of the houses he and Harry rob, so they can call themselves what?

    A. the Thirsty Thieves
    B. the Faucet Burglars
    C. the Wet Bandits
    D. the Sink Swindlers

19. According to the Guinness Book of World Records, how much did Home Alone gross worldwide?

    A. $350 million
    B. $423 million
    C. $512 million
    D. $533 million

20. TRUE OR FALSE:
Macaulay Culkin improvised the line, "You guys give up? Or are you thirsty for more?"

17.

B. eggnog

18.

C. the Wet Bandits

19.

D. $533 million

20.

TRUE

21. TRUE OR FALSE:

Daniel Stern had to step on real ornaments to film the scene where Marv sneaks in through the window.

22. TRUE OR FALSE:

The black and white movie Kevin watches, Angels with Filthy Souls, was a real movie.

23. TRUE OR FALSE:

The picture of "Buzz's girlfriend" was a picture of the art director's daughter.

24. TRUE OR FALSE:

Macaulay Culkin drew the map that Kevin uses to show where his traps are set up.

25. TRUE OR FALSE:

In the scene where the tarantula is on Marv's face, the scream heard from Daniel Stern was entirely real.

21.

FALSE: The "ornaments" were actually made of candy.

22.

FALSE: The "movie" was specially created for Home Alone, and was a play on the James Cagney film Angels with Dirty Faces.

23.

FALSE: Director Chris Columbus thought it would be cruel to make fun of an actual girl, so they used a picture of the art director's son made up to look like a girl.

24.

TRUE

25.

FALSE: Although he no doubt wanted to scream, Daniel Stern had to mime the scream when the tarantula was on his face. A real scream would've scared the spider, so the sound had to be dubbed in afterwards.

26. TRUE OR FALSE:
Macaulay Culkin was the only boy who auditioned for the role of Kevin.

27. TRUE OR FALSE:
Joe Pesci deliberately avoided Macaulay Culkin on the set to appear "mean" and add more realism to Culkin's performance.

28. TRUE OR FALSE:
At the beginning of the film, most of the shots of Macaulay Culkin are from above his head, making him appear smaller and weaker. But by the end of the movie, most of the shots are from below him, so he appears stronger and more confident.

29. TRUE OR FALSE:
The fake snow used in the movie was later given to a theme park.

30. Match the burglar to the trap that thwarted his efforts:

Falling clothes iron
Glue and feathers
Blowtorch to the head
Toy cars on the floor
Tarantula on the face

26.

FALSE: Although John Hughes specifically had Culkin in mind when he wrote the script, he auditioned several hundred other boys just to be sure he made the right decision.

27.

TRUE

28.

TRUE

29.

FALSE: The fake snow was given to the Lyric Opera of Chicago and has been used in numerous productions.

30.

Falling clothes iron (Marv)
Glue and feathers (Harry)
Blowtorch to the head (Harry)
Toy cars on the floor (both)
Tarantula on the face (Marv)

FROSTY THE SNOWMAN

1. What is the name of the magician the teacher hires to entertain the classroom?

    A. Professor Plum
    B. Magic Mike
    C. Professor Hinkle
    D. Doctor Magic

2. What Emmy-winning comedian narrates and sings the titular song?

    A. Jack Benny
    B. Jimmy Durante
    C. Wally Cox
    D. Burl Ives

1.

C. Professor Hinkle

2.

B. Jimmy Durante

3. Production company Rankin/Bass produced which other popular holiday television special?

    A. Rudolph the Red-Nosed Reindeer
    B. A Charlie Brown Christmas
    C. A Claymation Christmas
    D. A Garfield Christmas

4. When the children build a snowman together, they consider many names for him. Which of the following is not one of the names they consider?

    A. Tony
    B. Christopher Columbus
    C. Oatmeal
    D. Harold

5. What magical accessory animates Frosty?

    A. His pipe
    B. His carrot nose
    C. His broomstick
    D. His hat

3.

A. Rudolph the Red-Nosed Reindeer

4.

A. Tony

5.

D. His hat

6. What are Frosty's first words?

    A. "Merry Christmas!"
    B. "How ya doin'?!"
    C. "Happy birthday!"
    D. "Happy New Year!"

7. Why does Frosty need to travel to the North Pole?

    A. It's a warm day and he's beginning to melt
    B. He wants to help Santa Claus prepare for Christmas Eve
    C. His family is from the North Pole
    D. Karen has always wanted to visit Santa's workshop and she needs a chaperon

8. Why must Frosty, Hocus Pocus, and Karen sneak onto the train as stowaways instead of ticketed passengers?

    A. The conductor won't let a snowman on the train
    B. They don't have any money
    C. The train line doesn't sell tickets for the refrigerated boxcar
    D. They need to get on the train quickly to evade Professor Hinkle

6.

C. "Happy birthday!"

7.

A. It's a warm day and he's beginning to melt

8.

B. They don't have any money

9. Frosty and Hocus Pocus know they must enlist someone's help to get Karen back home so she doesn't freeze. Whom do they choose?

    A. The marines
    B. The President of the United States
    C. Santa Claus
    D. Karen's mother

10. Santa Claus tells Professor Hinkle he must write a phrase a hundred zillion times as penance for his bad behavior. What is the phrase?

    A. "I am very sorry for what I did to Frosty."
    B. "I will be a good magician."
    C. "Snowmen are people, too."
    D. "I won't take back my hat."

11. TRUE OR FALSE:
Karen gives Frosty his name.

12. TRUE OR FALSE:
Hocus Pocus is Professor Hinkle's dog.

9.

C. Santa Claus

10.

A. "I am very sorry for what I did to Frosty."

11.

TRUE

12.

FALSE: Hocus Pocus is a rabbit.

13. TRUE OR FALSE:
Professor Hinkle is happy to let Frosty keep his magical hat.

14. TRUE OR FALSE:
Once the traffic cop realizes he was talking to a snowman who had come to life, he swallows his whistle.

15. TRUE OR FALSE:
Frosty builds a fire in the woods for Karen to keep her warm.

16. TRUE OR FALSE:
Frosty and Karen discover a greenhouse where Karen can stay warm while they wait for Santa Claus.

17. TRUE OR FALSE:
Frosty returned every year with the magical Christmas snow.

13.

FALSE: Once he realizes his hat is truly magical, Professor Hinkle wants it back for himself.

14.

TRUE

15.

FALSE: Hocus Pocus asks the woodland animals to build the fire so Karen can stay warm and Frosty won't melt.

16.

TRUE

17.

TRUE

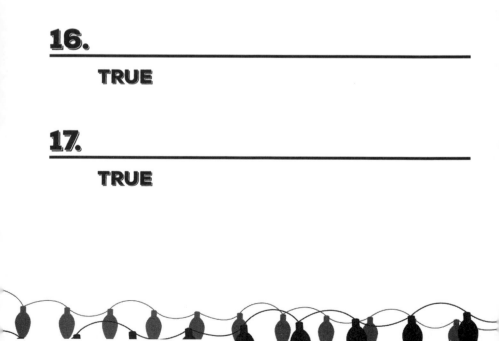

DIE HARD

1. What year was Die Hard released?

    A. 1986
    B. 1987
    C. 1988
    D. 1989

2. The director of the film had worked on another action flick, Predator, a year earlier. Who is he?

    A. John McTiernan
    B. Ridley Scott
    C. Renny Harlin
    D. David Fincher

1.

C. 1988

2.

A. John McTiernan

3. The action in Die Hard takes place during a Christmas party at what fictitious Los Angeles office building?

    A. Nagasaki Tower
    B. Nakatomi Plaza
    C. Nakatomi Tower
    D. Nagoya Plaza

4. Bruce Willis played John McClane, a New York City police detective. Why does McClane travel to Los Angeles on Christmas Eve?

    A. to finalize his divorce
    B. for vacation
    C. to spend Christmas with his kids
    D. to reconcile with his wife

5. Which of the following actors was NOT considered for the part of John McClane before it went to Bruce Willis?

    A. Arnold Schwarzenegger
    B. Richard Gere
    C. Mel Gibson
    D. Tommy Lee Jones

3.

B. Nakatomi Plaza

4.

C. to spend Christmas with his kids

5.

D. Tommy Lee Jones

6. What is the name of McClane's limo driver who gets trapped in the office building garage?

    A. Argyle
    B. Alex
    C. Albert
    D. Arnold

7. Which actress played McClane's estranged wife Holly?

    A. JoBeth Williams
    B. Mimi Rogers
    C. Linda Hamilton
    D. Bonnie Bedelia

8. When McClane visits his wife at her office, why do they argue?

    A. McClane forgot to bring Christmas gifts
    B. Holly ridicules McClane's job
    C. McClane is upset that Holly is using her maiden name
    C. Holly thinks McClane should have arrived earlier

6.

A. Argyle

7.

D. Bonnie Bedelia

8.

C. McClane is upset that Holly is using her maiden name

9. Which actor, who would later appear in the Harry Potter adaptations, played Hans Gruber, the lead terrorist who takes the party guests hostage?

 A. Alan Rickman
 B. Jason Isaacs
 C. Robbie Coltrane
 D. Michael Gambon

10. What do the terrorists say they are attempting to steal from the corporation?

 A. confidential information
 B. bearer bonds
 C. gold bars
 D. computer codes

11. What country are the terrorists from?

 A. Austria
 B. Hungary
 C. Germany
 D. Poland

9.

A. Alan Rickman

10.

B. bearer bonds

11.

C. Germany

12. How does McClane first try to get the attention of someone outside the building?

    A. he pulls the fire alarm
    B. he tries to call 911
    C. he throws office furniture through a window
    D. he shines flashlights at passing motorists

13. What is the name of the first terrorist who finds and confronts McClane?

    A. Fritz
    B. Tony
    C. Karl
    D. Uli

14. Which actor appears as Al Powell, the police officer who finally attempts to aid McClane?

    A. James Avery
    B. John Amos
    C. Ving Rhames
    D. Reginald VelJohnson

12.

A. he pulls the fire alarm

13.

B. Tony

14.

D. Reginald VelJohnson

15. What is Al buying at the store when he gets the call to check out the office tower?

    A. Twinkies
    B. Ho Hos
    C. Pop-Tarts
    D. a Snickers bar

16. How does McClane manage to get the attention of Al?

    A. fires a gun through a window
    B. lights some furniture on fire
    C. throws the body of a terrorist onto Al's car
    D. shines a flashlight in Al's eyes

17. Why does Al say he asked to be put on desk duty?

    A. he was injured
    B. he shot and killed a boy with a toy gun
    C. he likes paperwork
    D. he was tired of running after criminals

15.

A. Twinkies

16.

C. throws the body of a terrorist onto Al's car

17.

B. he shot and killed a boy with a toy gun

18. One of the hostages is much too arrogant and thinks he can outsmart the terrorists, with unfortunate results. What is his name?

    A. Robert
    B. Henry
    C. Harry
    D. Tom

19. How does McClane's limo driver, trapped in the parking garage, finally realize there's trouble in the office tower?

    A. he sees a terrorist in the garage
    B. someone shoots his limo
    C. he hears about it on the radio
    D. he turns on the TV in the limo

20. Who does Hans Gruber pretend to be when McClane discovers him and corners him?

    A. one of the hostages
    B. a police officer
    C. a maintenance worker
    D. the owner of the building

18.

C. Harry

19.

D. he turns on the TV in the limo

20.

A. one of the hostages

21. Why is Holly happy when one of the terrorists starts smashing decorations?

    A. she hates the decorations
    B. she knows he's angry because McClane is still alive
    C. she's hoping he'll stay distracted so some people can escape
    D. she thinks their plan has failed

22. What does Hans Gruber mockingly call McClane?

    A. a knight in shining armor
    B. a rogue cop
    C. a cowboy
    D. a hero

23. What classical piece is prominently featured throughout the movie?

    A. Mozart's 40th symphony
    B. Beethoven's 9th symphony
    C. Vivaldi's Four Seasons
    D. Beethoven's 5th symphony

24. TRUE OR FALSE:
Although the name of the office building in Die Hard was a work of fiction, the building itself actually exists – it is Fox Plaza on Avenue of the Stars in Los Angeles.

21.

B. she knows he's angry because McClane is still alive

22.

C. a cowboy

23.

B. Beethoven's 9th symphony

24.

TRUE

25. TRUE OR FALSE:

All of the actors who played the terrorists were actually German.

26. TRUE OR FALSE:

McClane took his shoes off when the terrorists attacked so he could quietly sneak up on them.

27. TRUE OR FALSE:

Die Hard was Alan Rickman's feature film debut.

28. TRUE OR FALSE:

Unlike most of the actors who played German-born terrorists in the movie, Bruce Willis was actually born in Germany.

29. TRUE OR FALSE:

Al Powell never shoots his gun in the movie.

25.

FALSE: Only a couple of the actors who played the German terrorists were German. The rest were chosen for their menacing looks – most of the actors were more than six feet tall.

26.

FALSE: A passenger on his plane to L.A. told McClane that the best way to relax after a long flight was to take your shoes off and bury your toes in the carpet. McClane was testing out his advice when the terrorists started shooting.

27.

TRUE

28.

TRUE

29.

FALSE: Al finally gets the courage to shoot again when he sees the terrorist Karl aiming an assault rifle at McClane.

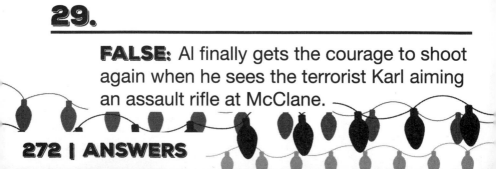